Explore Northumberland by Car

Explore Northumberland by Car

by
Jack Hanmer

Dalesman Books
1984

The Dalesman Publishing Co. Ltd.,
Clapham, via Lancaster LA2 8EB

First published 1984
© Jack Hanmer

ISBN: 0 85206 792 5

Printed by Alf Smith & Co., Bradford

Contents

Cover photograph of Bamburgh Castle by Tom Parker.

Introduction

THAT much overworked cliche 'County of Contrasts' befits Northumberland absolutely for it is exactly that. Its coastline is one of Britain's finest with off-shore islands by way of an added bonus. To the north, the Cheviots, heavy with sheep, stand sentinel twixt England and the auld enemy. The Pennine backbone with England's most famous footpath runs its entire north/south length, whilst Emperor Hadrian provided the east/west marker in the shape of his famous Wall.

Contained within this perimeter is a land rich in Christian, industrial and agricultural heritage which together with its turbulent history makes this a place to be expolored in every detail.

For convenience, the region has been divided into areas which could reasonably be explored from a central base. Alnwick, for example, would be ideal for the coastal strip (A) and Wooler for the Cheviot Border area (C). The second coastal strip (B) extends to Seaton Sluice and also includes Morpeth. Inland again and into thinly populated Redesdale and Coquetdale (D), with Rothbury and Otterburn to the north, and The Wall to the south. The last of these divisions (E) takes in the very latest tourist attraction lying north-west of Bellingham — Kielder Water.

Almost four hundred square miles of the county is designated a National Park and people who run such areas are committed to preserving the character of the landscape and promoting open air recreation. Whatever your particular interest, walking, ornithology, sailing, archaeology, photography or simply enjoying the countryside, you will find it within these bounds. Whether walking with the professionals along the bleaker stretches of the Pennine Way or a nature trail through a copse with the family, the opportunities are many and varied.

On a personal level, the people of Northumberland are a delight to meet and, like most rural folk, friendly and helpful. There will be whole chunks of conversation which you will miss for the accent is incredible, but do persevere for the colour of their speech contributes greatly to the whole Northumberland scene.

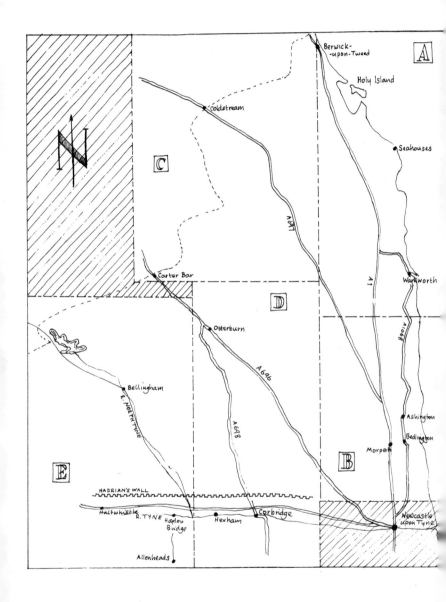

The places listed within these pages will help you to see much of what is best in the county, but you should delve deeper into the whole Northumberland story — particularly Border battles and Christian missions — to feel the real atmosphere. Here alas, we can only scratch the surface. Castles, pele towers, coastal villages, unique cattle, magnificent scenery, charming county towns and equally charming folk, all contribute to make Northumberland a delight to explore.

A. The Coast from Berwick to Amble

THE main artery, the Great North Road, A1, runs parallel to the coast with minor B class roads linking the coastal villages. Travelling north from Amble the views seaward are first of Coquet Island at the mouth of the Coquet, then the Farne Islands, haunt of seals and wild birds. After Bamburgh, the outline of Lindisfarne, Holy Island, fills the skyline whilst on the coast itself the castles of Warkworth, Dunstanburgh and Bamburgh loom large as though vying with each other for pride of place. A particular odour permeates the air around Craster when kippers are being cured in the local factory, whilst at Seahouses the boat men will seek your custom to ferry you across to the seals.

Inland the view west of the Cheviots; sheep rearing country traversed by lonely roads which meet the Wooler/Coldstream highway running on over the Border. Even in the height of summer these byways seem less busy than those in other parts of the county.

Berwick upon Tweed

BERWICK UPON TWEED belongs to the York and Chester league in that it is a walled town and, though lacking a cathedral or minster, Berwick's chequered history is probably unequalled in Britain, the town having changed hands innumerable times, so that it is no surprise to find that it is walled. In fact, it was twice walled!

Originally this was on the orders of Edward I and later on Elizabeth's as a protection, chiefly, against gun powder. It is this Elizabethan fortification which ranks amongst the finest in Europe, being in an excellent state of preservation and a two mile walk around the ramparts will confirm this. The former castle is now alas a railway station, and a plaque reveals that Robert the Bruce's claim to Berwick for Scotland was declined hereabouts.

The most dominant features of the town are the three bridges which cross, ironically, one of Scotland's best loved rivers, the Tweed. The first of these was the old stone bridge, 1634, costing a mere £15,000 and now replaced with a bland concrete structure, the Royal Tweed. Stephenson's Royal Border Bridge carried the railway line across the river which, when the tide is out, is a very muddy place.

Though very much England, Berwick's football team plays in the Scottish League, and the town is also home for the Regimental Museum of the Kings Own Scottish Borderers which is open to the public.

Amongst the more interesting buildings in the town, the National Trust has a watching brief over numbers 12, 13 and 20 Quay Walls which are fine examples from the Georgian period. Other buildings of note include the Guildhall, the Art Gallery Museum and Holy Trinity Church — reputedly one of only two churches built in Cromwell's time.

Crossing the old bridge brings you to Tweedmouth, the dock area, then Spittal where the lifeboat and the sailing club are to be found. A good stretch of fine sand has made Spittal Berwick's seaside resort with sea angling trips available from the pier.

Berwick's other role is that of springboard for excursions into the Border country.

Lindisfarne (Holy Island)

Nine miles south of Berwick on A1, signed Beal and Holy Island.

BEFORE crossing the three miles of causeway and sand flats from Beal, the tide table must be scrutinised carefully, for motorists are occasionally stranded by an incoming tide on the return journey. A rough rule is that crossing is impossible two hours before and three and a half hours after a high tide.

Missionaries from Iona came here in the seventh century, but by the ninth they had been driven out by the Danes. Today the ruins of an eleventh century priory and a sixteenth century castle are the reminders of previous occupations and both can be visited. In the early 1900s, Lutyens restored the castle for private occupation and in 1944 it was handed over to the National Trust.

St. Mary's Church stands by the Priory and here local brides jump over the 'petting stool' to bring them luck. For the naturalist the shallow tidal waters attract wild ducks, there is a wide variety of plant life on the dunes and the views across to the Farne Islands are excellent.

A curious feature of the tiny village are the tarred remains of former herring boats, now used as fishermen's huts. The geologist, the ornithologist and the mead drinker would be well pleased with

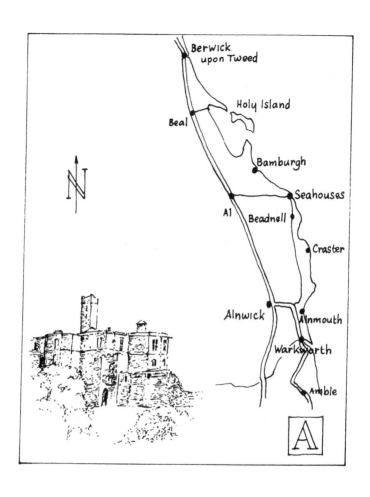

Lindisfarne, this latter commodity being produced locally alongside a local liqueur and honey.

As mentioned earlier, some preliminary reading will make any visit to Lindisfarne that much more interesting.

Bamburgh

Turn eastward off the A1, south of Belford onto the B1342 skirting Budle Bay.

PERHAPS the most photogenic building in Britain, particularly from the shoreline, is this imposing sandstone castle which dominates the picturesque village of Bamburgh. There are three attractions in the village: the castle, St. Aidan's Church and the Grace Darling museum. Now in the care of the Armstrong family, parts of the castle have been converted into flats, but the rest is open for viewing. Films and commercials have made use of its unique position, rising as it does on a pedestal of basalt rock above clear white sand.

The Parish Church, one of Northumberland's largest, has a beautiful thirteenth century chancel. The original building, erected in the seventh century, was used by St. Aidan as his base. Grace Darling's heroic sea rescue is well known and her boat, together with various artifacts, are in the local museum dedicated to her memory.

There are some popular parking spots in the sand dunes off a cul-de-sac running north and more parking places off the road south, running towards Seahouses. This minor road north leads to Harkness Rocks and the lighthouse. A footpath across the golf course takes you to Budle Bay, a haunt of wild fowl and in the safe keeping of the Nature Conservancy people. Not surprisingly, the view north is of Holy Island and its castle.

Bamburgh has no 'scars' for the architecture of the tiny village and the castle blend admirably.

Seahouses and Farne Island

Below Bamburgh on the B1340.

AFTER Bamburgh, the contrast is marked. This is a thriving place with two distinct faces: the harbour and the town. From the quayside you will be beckoned, enticed perhaps, to take a trip to the Farne Islands to view the seals and the bird life — eighteen different species in total.

Now in the care of the National Trust, all the information concerning the Islands and sailings is available at the harbour or the National Trust shop, 16 Main Street. There are some thirty of these rocky islands totalling about eighty acres and their most famous role is that of breeding ground for the grey seals. Bird life amongst these volcanic rocks includes cormorants, shags, puffins, gulls and terns. It was from Longstone Lighthouse that Grace Darling made her epic rescue.

Large fish lorries busy themselves around the harbour which is an interesting place, particularly when boats are returning. Some boat building might also be seen.

To succumb to general demand, the town has acquired the trappings of more famous seaside resorts, but this has not reduced its popularity. One can choose which facet of the town appeals most. It is a magnet in the holiday season, being the only place of its kind on this stretch of coast.

Beadnell

On the B1340 two miles south of Seahouses.

MUCH smaller than Seahouses, but a tiny picturesque harbour with cobles moored and old lime kilns at its head. An excellent information board, courtesy of the National Trust, reveals all to anyone unfamiliar with the workings of lime kilns. Sailing is very popular in Beadnell Bay and the skin diving centre is also located here. Parking is virtually impossible at the harbour, but a walk down is quite rewarding.

Low Newton by the Sea/Newton Haven

Take B1340 from Seahouses via Beadnell and Swinhoe. At junction with B1339 turn east to High Newton, then Low Newton.

THE off-shore reef at Newton Haven creates an almost perfect natural harbour where board sailing (wind surfing) is popular. Instruction is available for the novice. A square of quaint fishermen's houses provides the architectural interest in this tiny hamlet, where again parking can present a problem.

Embleton

On the B1339, the first village south of the junction with the B1340.

THE shoreline here is National Trust preserve and a coastal path enables you to walk, via Dunstanburgh Castle, to Craster. In the village, turn seaward towards the golf course, then south, keeping the castle in view. You can rendezvous with your driver in Craster village if you take the walk. The mile long sandy Embleton Bay, though not suitable for swimming, is the quiet sort of place one might choose for a picnic.

Nearby Newton Pool is a fresh water nature reserve purchased with the help of the World Wildlife Fund. Access is restricted to the edge of the reserve.

Craster

In Embleton village leave the B1339 and travel south on the minor road running nearer the coast. The approach from the Embleton/Howick road is through a castellated gateway, an eighteenth century folly.

CRASTER and kippers are synonymous. They are sent by post to friends and purchased at the factory for personal consumption by caravanners and self-catering holidaymakers. The harbour, like any other, is at its best on a full tide with its moored cobles awaiting another call to go fishing. On the skyline to the north is the expansive Dunstanburgh castle, its eleven acres standing atop the dolomite cliffs. To reach the castle, you walk on from the harbour.

In busier times Craster exported local basaltic rock, whinstone, but its current fame is based on the kipper industry and its appeal as a charming coastal fishing village. The car park is in the disused quarry on the edge of the village and an Information Centre, parked here in the season, is a useful port of call.

There is an interesting contrast between the colour of the two small off-shore islands, Muckle Carr and Little Carra, and the starker rock south of the harbour. From Craster a short diversion to Rock would not be out of place. It is an interesting example of an estate village with its quaint mid Victorian cottages and its hall which is now a Youth Hostel. A tiny, but lovely church, with twelfth century Norman arch contains a memorial to Charles Bosenquet who acquired the estate from the Royalist family, the Salkelds. It is located just off the B1340 about five miles north of Alnwick.

Howick Hall Gardens and Boulmer

On the minor coastal road just south of Craster.

AN HONESTY BOX at the gate requires you to deposit a modest fee to view these popular gardens which are open during the afternoon from April to September. Howick Hall (not open) was the home of Earl Grey, Prime Minister at the time for the Reform Bill. From the tiny hamlet it is possible to take the cliff path which runs north via Cullernose Point to Craster and south past Howick Haven some two miles to Boulmer. About a quarter of a mile inland from the Haven are the remains of a pre-historic settlement. At Boulmer, the only coastal habitation before Alnmouth, the RAF station dominates the village. A one-time haunt of smugglers, Boulmer Haven is now a peaceful place where local fishermen haul in their boats and unload their catch.

Alnmouth

The B1339 runs through Longhoughton, then Lesbury, where the B1338 runs seaward to the town.

TWO claims to fame: a golf course laid out in 1869 is thought to be one of England's oldest and since 1200 it has been a sea port. It was originally the port for Alnwick with the river navigable as far as Lesbury Bridge. During the eighteenth century grain was exported, but today it is known best as a yachting centre.

The most striking view is obtained from across the wide sweep of the Aln estuary when the town, perched on its south facing peninsula, is seen at its best. For those with an eye for interesting architecture, it is a fascinating exercise trying to identify former granaries which have long since been converted to private houses — the height and the small windows give them away.

There are donkey rides and the typical seaside refreshment kiosks on a very popular beach northside of this town which still retains an air of respectability. It is a pleasant place, as yet unspoiled by twentieth century so-called amenities.

Warkworth

On the A1068 coast road, two miles north of Amble.

LIKE Bamburgh it is the castle at Warkworth which dominates the village. From whichever approach, north or south, the view is impressive and perhaps even better from the far bank of the River Coquet.

With such illustrious names as King John, Hotspur and Shakespeare having associations with the castle, it is no surprise that its history is remarkable and certainly worth an hour's reading time. Running down from the castle is the eighteenth century village street with its cross and old bridge across the Coquet. Bridge End House by the fourteenth century bridge is a fine building and from here the composite view of river, street and castle can be enjoyed.

A truly beautiful, almost complete, Norman church, St. Lawrence's, has one of Northumberland's longest naves, some ninety feet.

You can row yourself or take a ferry trip up the wooded river to pass under the castle walls towards The Hermitage. Alternatively, a path from the castle takes you upstream to where the boatman will ferry you across the river to view this remarkable cave. Here you will find cell, dormitory, kitchen and chapel, all hewn out of solid rock and in use until the end of the sixteenth century.

A visit to Warkworth in spring will find the grassy slopes around the castle covered in daffodils. Dubbed one of Northumberland's finest attractions, this village and castle should not be missed.

Amble

South of Warkworth on A1068.

AMBLE-BY-THE-SEA lies on the south bank of the Coquet as it spills into the North Sea. It is the southernmost point of what is described as the Heritage Coast of Outstanding Beauty.

The drive from Warkworth follows the river and affords views of the town, the estuary and Coquet Island lying just off shore. Putting it kindly, Amble has seen better days in that when it prospered as a coal exporting port, it was a much busier place. Plans are afoot to recapture some of its former image and pleasure yachts now replace coal freighters, whilst some fishing boats still use the port.

A nineteenth century breakwater made the almost natural harbour even more usable and there now appears to be permanent activity around the harbour in an effort to improve again the facilities.

Being within striking distance of Tyne and Wear, the seaside aspect of the town is popular having a municipal-owned caravan site, good firm sands and a safe bathing beach at White House Sands. The golf course was apparently a Bronze Age burial ground and a variety of human remains and utensils have been unearthed. A low rainfall and a bracing climate are two assets which will please the holidaymaker.

Coquet Island is now inhabited by eider ducks, though it was formerly the site of a Benedictine Monastry. A lighthouse now occupies the site which will please mariners because the 'graveyard' tag was formerly applied to this hazardous stretch of coastline.

Alnwick

FOR many this is Northumberland's most interesting town on several counts. Its jewel is the castle, the seat of the historic house of Percy. Built on a twelfth-century site, it was restored in the eighteenth and nineteenth centuries by the Duke of Northumberland and today is one of England's treasures and much visited. To see it to advantage you should cross the Aln and climb towards the A1 but park in the lay-by and then look back to admire the almost identical view painted by Canaletto which now hangs in the castle.

The town is very much olde worlde and has suffered hardly at all from 'modern' planning. A history trail takes in over a dozen interesting features with architecture spanning more than three centuries.

On the southern approach to the town are two more striking features. The Percy Tenantry Tower, known locally as the 'Farmers' Folly', was erected in 1816 by grateful tenants who had received a reduction in rent! The Percy Lion with 'starched' tail stands atop the column. Closer to the town centre is the Hotspur tower through which the traffic passes. Of four such towers built when Alnwick was a walled town it alone survives, Hotspur being the 2nd Earl of Northumberland's father.

Equipped with the Town Trail guides issued by the Civic Society and information gleaned from the Tourist Office, you will find much to occupy you in Alnwick and its immediate surrounds. As a base from which sorties can be made into the surrounding area, Alnwick is ideal.

B. Morpeth, the Wansbeck, the Blyth and the Coast

THIS is the smallest section in area, but its lack of size has little bearing on the amenities it has to offer. 'Leisure' appears to be the key word and provision for the pursuit and enjoyment of it is quite generous. The area is bounded to the north by the huge sweep of Druridge Bay and to the south the Northumberland boundary has been re-drawn around Seaton Sluice to exclude the Novocastrians.

Two rivers, the Wansbeck and the Blyth, bisect the region and much of the provision for recreation is centred around them.

Morpeth is the focal point as any market day will confirm, but Ashington has a place in most people's memories as having something to do with football and the winning of coal. Speaking of which this is Miners' Gala land, the home of the famous terrier, memorials to politicians, strong links with George Stephenson and a Saxon church with a history of twelve hundred years of religious life.

Morpeth

Now by-passed by the A1; the A197 leads into the town, fifteen miles from Newcastle.

THE TOWN stands on a loop of the Wansbeck which is crossed by, as one has come to expect, one of Telford's bridges. The original thirteenth century one is now a footbridge and there are stepping stones for the adventurous — or foolhardy. Morpeth has suffered historically from its proximity to Newcastle in that, unlike Alnwick or Berwick, it never acquired that olde worlde air. Nevertheless, it does offer the visitor a number of interesting features, including a town hall designed by Vanbrugh and a number of churches which are worth visiting. High Church at the southern approach was originally the Parish Church and is one of Northumberland's finest. Its near neighbour is the battlemented court house and Police Station, mistaken by many to be the town's castle. This latter was originally a Norman construction restored in the fifteenth century. The Gatehouse which is all that has survived is a private residence.

The Chantry Museum is in an interesting part of the town, but currently it is undergoing restoration. Art lovers will find various temporary exhibitions in the Cameo Gallery in the King Edward VI School and old salts who acquired their nautical training at *HMS Collingwood* may like to know that Admiral Collingwood, who took over Nelson's command, was one of Morpeth's sons.

The town has an extremely well equipped Tourist Information Centre and information on the attractions of the surrounding area is readily available from an enthusiastic staff.

River Wansbeck

BETWEEN Kirkwhelpington and Morpeth the meanderings of this river are almost too numerous to count. It is depicted on the O.S. map as though it were something from the pages of a medical journal. The District Council has used the river to advantage in providing attractive walks and creating pleasing landscapes along its banks.

Around Bothal the river flows through a wooded gorge and there's a fourteenth century castle and a church. In today's economic

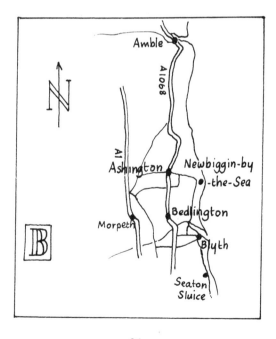

climate, castles are not the easiest of abodes to maintain, but at Bothal a local company has acquired this one for use by visiting dignitaries.

It would be difficult now to identify the numerous hamlets which were once a feature of this valley. They appear to have been absorbed in the inevitable development which has taken place in recent times.

The original weir at Sheepwash coincides with the tidal reach. A second weir some 1½ miles downstream is by the bridge which carries the spine road towards the Tyne tunnel. A good example of public relations is provided by the Wansbeck Riverside Park which has been developed by the Wansbeck District Council. There is a camping and caravanning area, places for picnics, a children's playground and walk-ways along both banks of the river. If you have an hour to spare the mile-long Nature Trail lists seventeen different items for you to observe. Nearby Jubilee Park which caters for the sailing, surfing and water skiing fraternities was developed from old colliery workings.

The Wansbeck flows into the sea between Newbiggin and Blyth, at Sandy Bay.

Ashington

On the A197 five miles east of Morpeth.

MOTORISTS travelling south on the M1 will be forgiven for thinking that every other National Express bus heading north appears to be going to Ashington. It is probably an association of ideas because the name Ashington, once unknown outside its native Northumberland, is now known the length and breadth of England as the home town of those famous footballing families, the Milburns and the Charltons. The cry 'Wor Jackie' is reminiscent of some ancient battle cry of marauding invaders, and indeed the two Jackies, Milburn and Charlton, often played havoc with opponents on the football field.

Ashington's industrial claim was for long that of the largest 'pit village' possibly in the world and, certainly, coal was king in these parts. In recent years the town's pit image has been replaced by a more contemporary aspect — witness the Riverside Country Park. Swimming baths, squash courts and the inevitable large shopping complex have helped to create new facets to the town.

Newbiggin by the Sea

On the coast via the A197 from Ashington (two miles).

NEWBIGGIN has no harbour as such, just a rough breakwater to protect a few local fishing boats — the cobles.

Its promenade was extended round the bay to the church point, but an erosion problem in these parts is something of a headache. There is a golf course and a caravan park and the District Council does endeavour to maintain the resort's status as a place for holidays.

Woodhorn Church

ABOUT a mile inland from the coast and on the A197 between Ashington and Newbiggin stands this interesting ecclesiastical building, reputed to be the oldest in Northumberland.

The original church dates from Saxon times and it is of remarkable interest especially to the historian who is able to see various types of architecture. These include Saxon, Norman, Gothic and some extensive renovations in the mid-1800s. It is now in the care of the Wansbeck District Council and is open Tuesday to Saturday, 10.00 a.m. to 12 noon, and 1.00 p.m. to 4.00 p.m.

The River Blyth

THIS is the second of the two major rivers which bisect the area and it enters the sea after passing between North Blyth and Blyth itself. It is crossed by two ferries for foot passengers, the old chain ferry for cars having been discontinued many years ago.

Where the river flows from Bedlington is the Plessey Woods Country Park. This is a spot which is repeated many times over in similar locations up and down the country — an oasis of tranquility where bluebells carpet the woods and pleasant evenings are taken. Hartford Hall stands on the northern bank of the river and today serves as a miners' rehabilitation centre. In 1832 a certain Mr. Hodgson described it thus: 'like a jewel in a diadem of enchantment glittering around beautiful woods and grounds,' and perhaps today those who know it would not disagree.

Flowing between steep banks as it does in these parts, the river tends to preserve the illusion of rural charm. The Riverside Nature Trail between Humford Mill and Attlee Park is another of the Council's endeavours to this end.

Bedlington

On the A1068 four miles south-east of Morpeth.

THIS is another one of those names which 'rings a bell', this time with memories of the famous Bedlington terrier. Historians will remember the town for its connections with the great George Stephenson; the old Bedlington Iron Works made the rails and the dogs (nails) for his tracks and locomotives were made at the local foundry. Ironically, genuine 'horse power' was required to pull the engines up Furness Bank!

The annual miners' gala has been held at either Ashington or more recently in Attlee Park, Bedlington.

The broad Front Street of the town which leads down to the river has such a variety of architectural styles that it has been designated a conservation area. Two other points of interest concerning Bedlington: it was until 1884 in the County Palatine of Durham and St. Cuthbert's Church confirms that the Saint's body passed this way.

Blyth

On the A193 eight miles south-east from Morpeth.

SUB-MARINERS will remember Blyth in its role as a war-time submarine base and schoolboy statisticians will have it recorded as Britain's main coal exporting port. Today there are no submarines but coal, on a much reduced scale, is exported. its imports include timber and paper and it is the Alumina Terminal for the giant Alcan empire. Roll-on roll-off facilities are imminent.

The old lighthouse — built for some obscure reason in a back street — is no longer in use and new lights adorn the harbour entrance. As with Newbiggin the Council has endeavoured to capture a resort atmosphere with its long beach of whitish sand, swimming pool, sailing club, golf — real and mini, and the usual array of amenities which constitute a place where you can take the children for the day. A Railway Museum in the local school lays special emphasis on the Blyth and Tyne Railway and is open most Monday evenings.

The face of Northumberland — ploughland patterns in the landscape near Rothbury *(Geoffrey N. Wright).*

By the coast. Above: Berwick upon Tweed, showing the old bridge linking the town with Tweedmouth *(British Tourist Authority)*. **Opposite — Top:** **Lindisfarne and its sixteenth century castle** *(Northumberland Gazette)*. **Bottom: The harbour at Craster, an old-world fishing village** *(Edwin Mitchell)*.

Northumberland castles. Above: Norham, west of Berwick, built in the twelfth century and last attacked in 1530 *(Geoffrey N. Wright)*. **Opposite — Top: Bamburgh, one of the most photogenic buildings in Britain** *(Geoffrey N. Wright)*. **Bottom: Horses at grass provide a sense of scale for Alnwick's majestic ramparts** *(British Tourist Authority)*.

Contrasting scenes near Wooler. Above: Panorama over the valley of the River Till from Old Bewick Hill *(Geoffrey N. Wright)*. Opposite — Top: Picturesque dovecot and impressive cloud patterns *(Geoffrey N. Wright)*. Bottom: Four members of the famous herd of Chillingham Wild Cattle *(Northumberland Gazette)*.

Hadrian's Wall: foundations of the granary at Housesteads Fort, looking east
(Geoffrey N. Wright).

Lynemouth and Ellington

On the coast east of the A1068 seven miles from Morpeth.

THESE neighbouring villages developed as the local collieries grew and the original separation of the workers from the management can be seen in the planning of both the area and the houses. Today the emphasis has moved from mine to smelter with the giant Alcan works on the doorstep.

When the two mines merged in 1983 the tag 'largest under-the-sea coal mine' became appropriate. There is evidence of coal along some of the cliff faces and in places where seams come to the surface on the sea bed, hence the local pastime of sea coal gathering.

Just north-east of Ellington is Cresswell — a name derived from locally grown watercress — and by crossing the links here the southern tip of sandy Druridge Bay is reached.

Seaton Sluice

On coast three miles south of Blyth.

This is the southern extremity of the new Northumberland. The name derives from the sluice which was built to clear sand deposited by the tides. The harbour, which once exported coal, was built by Sir Ralph Delaval in the late seventeenth century and cutting through solid rock in those days would have been no easy task. Today it is now being developed as a small boat marina. Sir Ralph's family seat, Seaton Delaval Hall, stands about a mile inland and was designed by Vanbrugh in 1720. It is a fine example of English baroque and is open to the public on Wednesday and Sunday afternoons.

Another Vanbrugh building in the village is the Octagon, thought to have been the Harbour Master's house, but today not serving any purpose.

Bolam

Lies between Whalton and Hartburn, eight miles west of Morpeth.

THE Bolam Country Park boasts an Information Centre which opens for an hour before noon and for another hour from 3.00 p.m. to 4.00 p.m. There is on display a graphic representation of the geology and natural history of the area. Bolam has been described as a medieval deserted village which is exactly what it is — the church and the Hall being the only two places which still survive. The Hall is now a gatehouse but the church can be visited and, being described as one of the few well preserved Saxon churches in Northumberland, it does have a certain pull.

C. Border Country —
Inland from Berwick to the heart of
the Cheviots

THERE are two quite distinct faces to this vast thinly populated area, each in its own special way having enormous appeal.

First, the intimate villages and the market town, and second, the wild expanse of nothingness which has more sheep to the square mile than humans. In spite of the obstacles which the military are obliged to put in the tourists' way, and the rationing of passes to one secret valley, visitors to the area appear to delight in what they see and certainly return for a second look.

Walkers have a wide choice of terrain and the person who seeks out the unusual will have a field day. With unique wild cattle, huge murals, historic bridges and battle grounds, the choice is indeed a wide one.

There are a number of interesting villages associated with the Tweed and the Till and it is convenient to follow their respective courses in order not to miss anything.

Horncliffe

A village lying north of the A698 some five miles west from Berwick.

THE main attraction here is nearby Union Bridge which transports the traveller from England to Scotland as he crosses the Tweed. It was the first vehicular suspension bridge in Britain and its wrought-iron links have earned it the name 'Chain Bridge.' Picnicking under the bridge on the English bank of the river is popular and certainly very pleasant.

The village of Horncliffe stands on a high bank by a wide sweep of the Tweed and the footpath from the foot of the glen takes you to Norham Castle.

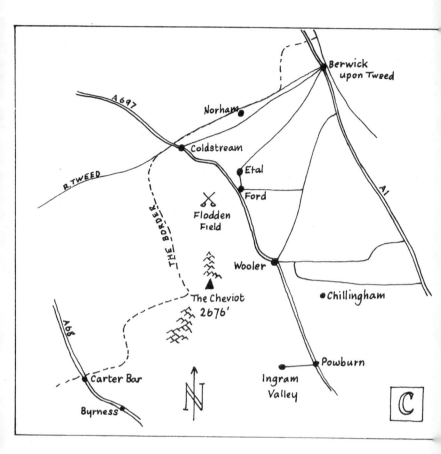

Norham

Six miles along the A698 Coldstream Road from Berwick, then west on the B6470.

THE layout of Norham village is reminiscent of Warkworth with its ancient castle standing sentinel at one end, the church at the other and a river connecting the two. The head of the Tweed's tideway is also hereabouts. The long main street leads down from the castle to an elongated triangle of a village green, and the lane which leads off to the river and the church dating originally from the mid-eight hundreds.

For four hundred years the castle was attacked, demolished, restored and beseiged, in that order, by both warring factions. Built early in the twelfth century, its role in Border battles was played out from the reigns of Edward I to Henry VIII, it being last attacked in 1530. The strategic position of the village caused it to be the centre of the struggle which at the time brought about the desecration of this lovely valley of the Tweed.

Twizell Bridge

Three miles beyond Norham on the A698 before Cornhill.

THE River Till is the English tributary of the Tweed and the bridge has a significant place in history. The one bold, high stone arch is being replaced by a more modern and less pleasing concrete structure. It is thought by historians that the Battle of Flodden was really lost at Twizell. The English artillery crossed, literally under the noses of James IV's army, and then dominated the battlefield some three miles away. The ruins of eighteenth century Twizell Castle lie on the site of an earlier castle destroyed in 1496 by the same James.

Branxton for Flodden Field

A697 south from Coldstream or Cornhill, then minor road right signed Branxton.

THIS historic field is well signed from Branxton village and a short climb up the hill takes you to the monument. Here it was that in 1513 'all the flower of Scotland died on Branxton Hill'. James IV and several thousand of his kinsmen were slain in what has been described as the bloodiest of battles on English soil.

Ford and Etal

On B6353 and B6354 east of Crookham A687 Wooler road.

A SHORT diversion from the Wooler/Coldstream highway will bring you to these interesting villages. Ford Castle is now an educational establishment and not open, but the former village school is and should be visited. On the walls of the school, now the Lady Waterford Hall, are Biblical murals which Her Ladyship painted, using local villagers as her models. The caretaker will open the hall and give you an informative commentary.

The craft shop in this estate village is located by the Waterford fountain and the range includes pottery, wrought ironwork, poker work and paintings. Afternoon teas are available in the local Post Office and Northumbria Nurseries which are in the walled garden of Ford Castle produce beautiful ornamental trees and shrubs.

Travelling from Ford, B6353 to Etal, B6354, you pass on your right the prancing horses atop the gateway, then Heatherslaw Mill, a nineteenth century water-driven corn mill which still grinds flour. Adjoining the mill is High Kiln Crafts and the Granary Cafe offers home made teas.

Etal is on the Till, sometimes raging and sometimes slow moving. There is a crossing which tractors will negotiate with ease, but a car could well become waterlogged!

The village appears out of place having beautiful thatched cottages more in keeping with Devon or Dorset. Again, there are places to visit: the thatched *Black Bull* serves lunches and evening snacks and hand-made furniture is produced in the Old Power House by the river.

Dominating the village are the castle ruins, a fourteenth century structure and one of many which James IV laid waste en route to Flodden. The parish church stands in the grounds of Etal Manor, just across the main road.

At Letham Hill, near Crookham, is the Errol Hut Smithy and Workshop, where spinning wheels are made and lessons in spinning given.

The Ford and Etal estates are owned by Lord Joicey and a comprehensive leaflet describing all these attractions is available from most local Information Centres.

Kirk Yetholm

On B6401 south of Coldstream

THIS is by way of an intrusion for we are now in Scotland. Since the Pennine Way runs entirely through the Northumberland National Park, it would not be amiss to seek out its northern terminus. In practice, many more peoeple are likely to view its southern tip at Edale in the much visited Hope Valley. A cottage in Kirk Yetholm village recalls that this was the headquarters of Scottish gypsies until the late 1800s. The last of the Gypsy Queens described the scattered village in derogatory terms as having been 'built on a dark night'.

Wooler

On the A697 Coldstream-Morpeth road.

THIS is the largest market town in these parts and, like many such places, has seen better days in that it was, in the thirteenth century, the seat of a baron. The mound of the Norman castle which once guarded the southern approaches lies below the market place. Its cattle and sheep fairs were well known and an auction mart still operates.

The town lies on the edge of the National Park and some four hundred square miles of open country to the west make it a popular place for the hill walker and the angler. At Langleeford, five miles south-west, is perhaps the easiest of the approaches to the summit of The Cheviot, 2,676 feet. The views from the top are fitting reward for the effort put into the climb.

Agriculturally speaking, the town is very well endowed, and sheep are not the only product of these parts. There are a number of interesting excursions which can conveniently be made from Wooler, the most famous of which will be to the Chillingham Wild Cattle. This unique herd has been roaming the three hundred acres of parkland at Chillingham for centuries and in the early 1200s it was completely isolated from the outside world, thus ensuring its protection from foot and mouth disease. The cattle can be viewed by joining the parties which are escorted by one of the wardens from his cottage by the church. The church is worth visiting and contains the beautifully carved tomb of Sir Ralph Grey, the first owner of the castle, and his wife.

Also from Wooler you may obtain a 'permit to visit' College Valley and this can be collected from the Estates Office at 18 Glendale Road. Daily visitors to this remote valley are kept to a maximum of twelve to avoid overcrowding. It is, in fact, very remote with the odd isolated shepherd's cottage the only sign of human habitation. Take the B6351 at Akeld, north of Wooler. After Kirknewton, turn left for Hethpool, then just go ahead on a very minor road where picnicking by the rushing stream is possible. Take the right fork to the end of the road and walk on to view the Hen Hole if you have an hour to spare.

Other places of interest around Wooler are the Harthope and Happy valleys, both lying south and within walking distance. Doddington, three miles north, has an interesting church, and Dod Law rising above the village has ancient earth works and enclosures. A mile beyond Yeavering on the B6351, north of Wooler, is the site of the Saxon town Gefrin, and opposite is Yeavering Bell, the largest of Northumberland's Iron Age forts.

Ingram Valley

North of Powburn on west side of A697 minor road signed Brandon.

FOLLOW the line of the river Breamish below Brandon Hill where Bronze Age relics have been found. At Ingram village is a Mountain Rescue post and a National Park Information Centre. This attractive valley, a popular tourist spot, is a cul-de-sac with access on foot into the Cheviots, and the further west you travel, the more barren is the scenery and the purer is the air. The road leaves the river and climbs Greenside Hill to reach the hamlet of Hartside, the end of the line for motorists. Walkers may continue to Linhope Farm, then Linhope Spout which has the reputation of being one of Northumberland's prettiest waterfalls.

Whittingham and Callaly Castle

West of A697 south of Powburn.

THE River Aln divides this charming village in two, with the church on the north bank and the village green on the south. It is the only place of any size in the upper reaches of the Aln and again has seen much of the Border clashes, hence its two pele towers, though only one now remains standing. There have been numerous abortive attempts to restore it and put it to other more practical use, but it still stands, in need of some attention.

There is an interesting community service project based in the village. The Northumbria Police run an outdoor pursuit expedition centre for city youngsters. The best way to see the place, which now has a blend of the old and the new in its domestic architecture, is to leave the car in one half and cross the river on foot.

Nearby Callaly Castle has been the home of the Claverings for centuries and at the time of their possession of Warkworth Castle they were among those who opposed King John. The original thirteenth century building was a pele tower which was added to in the seventeenth and eighteenth centuries eventually becoming an extremely gracious mansion, with a variety of styles including the classical, Georgian and Victorian. It is in a lovely setting with the gardens being of particular interest.

Holystone, Harbottle and Alwinton

West of Rothbury, B6341, and north of Hepple.

IT IS convenient to consider these three villages together since they are invariably visited in this order. They lie at the head of Coquetdale and between them present an interesting picture of times past.

First Holystone with its Lady's Well, a pure spring, where St. Ninian baptised some 3,000 converts. The spring, incidentally, is the local water supply. It is a peaceful setting behind the *Salmon Inn*, which appropriately is a hostelry well favoured by anglers.

Harbottle lies under massive crags where stand boulders thrown up by some prehistoric volcano. The Drake or Dragon Stone stands near a lake in the Harbottle Hills and affords excellent views of the surrounding countryside. The ruins of the twelfth century castle are on a green mound by the village and its place in history concerns James I of Britain. His grandmother, the daughter of Margaret Tudor, was born there in 1515.

There is a National Park Information Centre at Harbottle Crags Nature Trail which lies on the stretch between Harbottle and Alwinton and is one of the starting points for the popular Discovery Walks. The Warden here will advise you about the military ranges beyond Alwinton. Before entering the village, look in at the church right which has an unusual design. Being on sloping ground, the chancel and the altar are higher than the nave and steps must be climbed to reach them.

The village of Alwinton stands at the confluence of the Coquet and Alwin, and the houses which have stood on the green haugh between the two rivers have changed little over the years. Although it is possible to motor on for a few more miles and in theory link up with the Scottish highway at Byrness, it is not usually convenient since the red flag which indicates 'firing in progress' is invariably flying. Nevertheless, the run up into the hills as far as one is permitted appears to be a popular one.

Clennell Street, one of the ancient Border routes, starts from Alwinton. It is a good day's walk over rough terrain reaching the actual border at Russell's Cairn, high on Windy Gyle at 2,032 feet.

One interesting feature of the area is the postal mini-bus which runs from Rothbury and serves these isolated villages which are devoid of public transport. There are other such services in rural Northumberland and information about them can be obtained from the Head Postmaster at Morpeth.

Byrness

On the A68 south of Carter Bar, the boundary between England and Scotland.

AT FIRST GLANCE this isolated village on the main route to Scotland has little to offer. It is somewhat deceptive for its facilities include a National Park Information Centre, a Youth Hostel, a caravan site nearby and the start of a scenic twelve mile Forest Drive. Motorists touring this region will find this Forest Drive to or from Kielder worth making.

Byrness is a Forestry Commission village within the Borders Forest region and the area caters, as one might expect, for the outdoor type.

In the local churchyard is a memorial to the men who died constructing the Catcleugh Reservoir about one mile nearer Carter Bar. It was, when finished, the largest stretch of water in the county, but today Kielder is much bigger.

D. Rothbury, Corbridge and Hadrian's Wall

WHEN huge tracks of a county are full of apparent 'nothingness' it comes as a pleasant surprise to light upon such charming places as Rothbury or Blanchland. They fall into a special category in that no other place is quite like them as we shall see later.

The Army has again been busy erecting their red danger flags on wild windswept moors. Perhaps history is repeating itself for Otterburn is a place mentioned frequently in military annals. The county border estends through Roman Corbridge to the River Derwent around Blanchland, after crossing what must be Britain's best known 'fence', Hadrian's Wall — more of which in the next chapter.

Rothbury

Lies west on the A697 and at the crossroads of the B6341, B6342 and B6344.

INVARIABLY dubbed Capital of Coquetdale, Rothbury is best described as a large, pleasant village wherein about 2,000 souls reside. It presents a very pleasing aspect, the long main street being on two levels with many of its shops on the 'high row' leading down to a small triangular green. An assortment of chestnut, ash and sycamore add to the general air of a place with some character. The National Park Information Centre in Church Street should be visited first in order to see at a glance what delights the area has in store for you. This will correct the misconception that there may not be much to do in these parts. Tourists who make Rothbury a base for a short stay can walk, fish, tour by car or delve into history. Rothbury's thirteenth century All Saints Church was largely restored in 1850 but it contains one of our finest examples of Saxon carving dating from the 800s.

Between Thropton and Rothbury are The Terraces, formed as a result of glacial action. At Old Rothbury and West Hill there were prehistoric forts and early settlements and less than a mile from the town bridge is the Thrum Gorge where the Coquet has gouged a narrow channel through the sandstone.

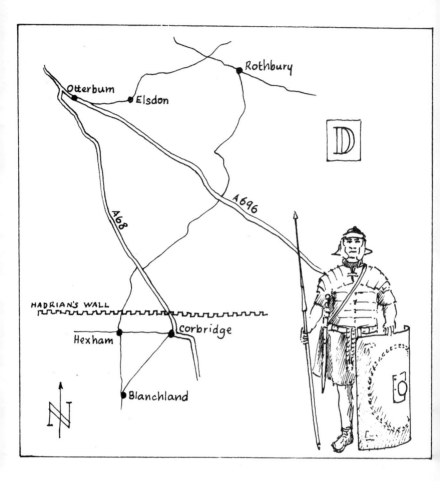

On the south side of the village lie the Simonside Hills where gentle walks are possible and the views are extensive. The Forestry Commission has provided a picnic area, car park and Nature Trail and leaflets on these and other local walks are usually available in newsagents and the Information Centre.

Rothbury is not the kind of place which you can see on your way through; it has to be explored at leisure to be appreciated.

Cragside

About a mile along the Alnwick Road, B6341.

LORD Armstrong's former estate is now in the care of the National Trust. Whilst architecturally it might best be described as a 'hotch potch' it is certainly worth a visit, either to stroll in the formal gardens or to visit the very interesting house which is claimed to be the first in the world to be lit by hydro-electricity. Lord Armstrong will be remembered for his work on hydraulics, guns, war ships and his various inventions, and to visit the thirty odd rooms open to the public is quite rewarding.

Brinkburn Priory

Lies on the Morpeth Road, B6344, south-west of Rothbury and still on the Coquet.

THE entrance lies about a mile beyond the curiously named village, Pauperhaugh, and before motoring down the drive to the Priory you are invited to 'pick your own' for this is soft fruit territory.

The Priory was founded in the 1100s, but by the mid 1800s it was in a very poor state. Some extremely skilful restoration work was carried out and today the Church of St. Peter and St. Paul reflects Norman architecture to a very high standard.

Elsdon

Take the B6341 through Thropton with Tosson Hill at 1,444 feet and Harwood Forest on your left.

THE valley of the Elsdon Burn takes you into Redesdale and its once Norman capital. Elsdon is another example of a strategically placed village and it is no surprise to find the whole area dotted with ruined pele towers. The walls of the fortified parsonage are eight feet thick. Lawlessness appeared to be the order of the day in these parts and the history of Redesdale is a colourful, though albeit confusing one. The large village green suggests both a meeting place and a gathering ground for cattle — hence the pinfold. It was also on an old drovers' route and its church, St. Cuthbert's, was supposedly one of the many resting places of that saint's body. Some two centuries ago the distinction of being Redesdale's capital passed to Otterburn. In spite of George Chatt's descriptive verse, Elsdon is a place worth seeing:

Hae ye ivver been at Elsdon?
The world's unfinish'd neuk
It stands amang the hungry hills
An' wears a frozen leuk.

Otterburn

Stands on the A696, just below its junction with the A68 at Elishaw.

THOUGH not a large place, it is popular with tourists and *The Percy Arms* suggests a staging post over many years. National Park and Border Forest areas to the north have helped to foster its popularity as an area in which walking, fishing and observing wild life can be pursued. The famous Otterburn battle in 1388 saw the Scots under Douglas defeat the Percys, and the Cross in a wooden plantation three quarters of a mile from the village commemorates this event. Just along the B6320 Bellingham Road is the 150 year old mill where the usual assortment of knitted goods may be purchased. The Roman Dere Street runs through these parts, and at Rochester the porch of the little school contains stone brought from Bremenium. This latter was a Roman fort at High Rochester and now forms part of the village green.

Today the presence of a more modern Army in the area has restricted access to much of the Roman heritage, but local guide books will point you in the direction of what can still be seen.

If you have an enquiring mind, you could locate Evitstones Bastle on the west side of the River Rede near Horsley. Only one of the original Bastle houses remains, as too does the question: 'why were they built there in the first place?'

Cambo and Wallington Hall

One the B6742, just north of its junction with the A696.

CAMBO is an estate village built in the mid-eighteenth century as an example of a model village and it was then associated with the Wallington estate. The grounds and the walled garden are open all year round, the house only from April to September. Built in 1688 by a Newcastle merchant, Sir William Blackett, Wallington is one of the largest properties to be administered by the National Trust. It contains the usual assortment of fine pictures, furniture and plaster work and, as an added bonus, collections of dolls' houses and coaches and a museum.

Rothley Crags and Rothley 'Castle'

AFTER Cambo, turn right onto the B6343 to Scots Gap, then left up to Rothley Crags, once a deer park and still within the bounds of the estate. The twin towers of Rothley Castle and the 'ruined' Mow Cop in Cheshire have much in common for they were both built as ruins! — the former decorative folly, the latter to mark the boundary of an estate. A switchback minor route returns to the B6342 and north to Rothbury.

Corbridge

Lies on the A68, south of the B6318 which follows the line of Hadrian's Wall.

ONCE the capital of Northumbria, this town has played an important role in the county's history since about AD 81 when the Romans developed it as a place to cross the Tyne and a junction for their Dere Street and Stanegate. The camp was at Corstopitum. Today the approach to Corbridge is across a seventeenth century bridge to an intriguing street plan with old market square, antique and craft shops, and an importnt church to complete the picture. St. Andrew's is probably as good an Anglo Saxon survivor as any you may find in the county, and adjacent to it the Vicar's Pele Tower now dispenses information.

Corbridge is one of those peculiar places which appear to draw people who may not be even remotely interested in Roman history. For those who are, the camp and museum are open daily and the line of the famous Wall lies some few miles north at Stagshaw Bank.

(The more exposed and better known sections of the Wall are described in the next chapter.)

Blanchland

On the Durham border south of Corbridge, the B6307, then B6306.

THE minor roads through Riding Mill and Slaley are probably even more hair-raising than the roller coaster route along the B6306. The village can rightly be described as unique in that no other place will compare exactly. Briefly, it developed from the Abbey founded in 1139, the stone cottages of the village proper being constructed later to house local lead miners. There are two 'entrances' — through the old gate house or across the old bridge over the Derwent. The hostelry, the *Lord Crewe Arms,* is an interesting place with a strong Jacobite connection, and a secret chamber in a chimney piece. The whole village has all the marks of a film set and like Castle Combe in Wiltshire is more in keeping with fairy tales than twentieth century hustle and bustle. The camera is very much in evidence in Blanchland.

The waters of the Beldon Burn mark the actual county boundary which also runs through the middle of the Derwent Reservoir one mile to the east. A perimeter road enables the tourist to drive (preferubly anti-clockwise direction) right round the reservoir which has been developed by the authorities as a tourist attraction. There are two picnic areas, at Millshield and Carricks, and a Country Park at Pow Hill. Fishing and sailing are also permitted.

E. Kielder Water, Hexham and more of Hadrian's Wall

WHILST this section might claim to be wilder and more thinly populated than the rest of Northumberland, it does contain two of Britain's most famous landmarks. To the north the recently constructed Kielder Water has transformed the landscape whilst to the south and running across its width about the same latitude as Newcastle is Hadrian's Wall. The largest town is Hexham and the contrast between it and, for example, Allenheads, could not be more marked. The Pennine Way which runs through Bellingham brings the hardy into these desolate parts of Northumberland. It is not difficult to appreciate why the region is now so thinly populated, except of course for cattle and sheep. Time was when coal mining and iron making held sway, but those days have long gone and today farmers and tourism are the chief industries. A similar scene unfolds to the south around Allendale, formerly a busy lead mining centre. The chief attraction is Hadrian's famous Wall, and it is in this region that it us seen at its best, together with the forts and other evidence of Roman occupation.

Kielder

North-west of Bellingham, a minor road after Falstone, leading to the B6357 and Hawick.

THE harnessing of the North Tyne has put Kielder into the record books as Europe's largest man-made lake. Whatever the arguments for and against changing the face of the beautiful countryside, it has to be admitted that scenically this is pleasing to the eye. There appears to be a happy compromise between man's need for water and his desire to pursue his pleasures. The Forestry Commission Information Centre at Kielder Castle and the Water Operations Centre at Tower Knowe, Falstone, should both be visited if detailed information on the whole area is required. At Kielder a popular twelve mile Forest Drive takes you over to Byrness on the Carter Bar road. Rising to 1,400 feet and passing the hill, Oh Me Edge, it is for most of its length unmetalled but quite useable and extremely scenic. About half a mile below Kielder village you should locate the old railway viaduct and

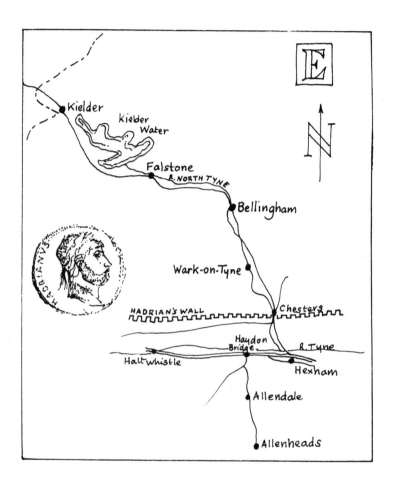

E

N

Kielder

Kielder Water

Falstone

R. NORTH TYNE

Bellingham

Wark-on-Tyne

HADRIAN'S WALL

Chesters

Haydon Bridge

R. Tyne

Halt Whistle

Hexham

Allendale

Allenheads

HADRIANVS

note how the waters of the new Bakethin Reservoir lap the supports. Concrete feet now preserve the stone work on this fine example of a skew bridge.

Motoring is only possible along the western shore where recreational facilities have now been provided. These include picnic sites, view points, boat launching areas, fishing and even swimming.

The villages of Falstone and Greenhaugh lie between the dam and Bellingham.

Bellingham

On the B6320 west of the A68.

THIS village of about 1,000 inhabitants must seem like an oasis to walkers on the Pennine Way or tourists who have crossed the Cheviots. Entering from the Kielder Road, you will meet St. Cuthbert's Church and the old gun. The church was yet another resting place for St. Cuthbert en route for Durham and its unusual stone roof was a result of raiders constantly burning the original wooden one. Behind the church is St. Cuthbert's Well — locally Cuddy's Well — with the inevitable healing waters.

The gun which is proudly displayed outside the Town Hall was rescued and brought back from the Chinese Boxer Rising. A Boer War memorial stands in the tiny market place and a Youth Hostel provides much needed rest for those on foot. The local Information Office, though small, is very efficient and a local pamphlet describes seven walks to places like the Blue Heaps, the bridges, the golf course and the 30 foot high Hareshaw Lynn — best viewed after a heavy rainfall.

Spoil heaps and mine shafts on the hills which surround the village are reminders of former days when farming was not the only activity in these parts.

Wark

On the B6320 south of Bellingham.

WARK stands on the North Tyne which is particularly attractive and crossed here by an impressive bridge. it was formerly the capital of North Tynedale but that honour now belongs to Bellingham. There is a colourful history of Scottish kings holding court in Wark together with detailed accounts of reiving and lawlessness which was a feature of such places. As far back as AD 788 King Alfwald of Northumbria was murdered in Wark. Today it is probably not given a second glance unless the traveller makes a point of running through the square. A sixteenth century farm house was converted into the *Battlesteads Inn,* an exercise which must have brought much relief to the local population. By crossing the bridge it is possible to motor down to Chollerford in the area of the Chesters Roman Cavalry Fort.

Hadrian's Wall

Between Newcastle and Carlisle north of the A69.

THERE are still those who see Hadrian's Wall as the boundary between England and Scotland and it is something of a surprise to discover that its eastern end is as far south as Newcastle, at Wallsend — where else? 'Hadrian was the first to build a wall, eight miles long, to separate the Romans from the Barbarians.' So reads the ancient reference to this magnificent achievement.

There are probably two kinds of visitor to The Wall: the tourist who recognises it as being a part of Britain's heritage and therefore puts it on his list of places he must visit, and the serious scholar who is, to whatever degree, interested in Roman history. On this latter point The Wall has become a mecca for parties of school children and students who are studying it in their syllabus.

The first call should be made at the very efficient Information Centre at Once Brewed on the Military Road, the B6318, or at one of the museums in Carlisle or Newcastle. A commerical venture in the form of an audio/visual presentation is available at Greenhead, also on the Military Road.

Thus equipped you are more likely to see the more interesting sections of The Wall and if time is limited this will ensure it is used to advantage. Briefly, the attractions which lie within this section are the exposed portions of The Wall and the various forts, garrisons, milecastles and hospital. Specifically and running from east to west they commence with Chesters, which has extremely well preserved remains of a cavalry fort, together with an excellent museum. Housesteads is very popular since it is the only example of a Roman hospital in Britain and it boasts a flushing latrine; also the views of The Wall as it dips and rises across the barran landscape are extremely good around Housesteads. Vindolanda, just before the Information Centre at Once Brewed, was a fort on the old Stanegate frontier. A civilian settlement was excavated on this site thus providing further interest. Like Chesters, there is also a small museum.

Devotees of the Pennine Way will know the three mile stretch westwards from Once Brewed where The Wall reaches its highest point on Winshields Crag, 1,230 feet, and walkers pass Milecastles 40, 41 and 42, this last one being Cawfields and again worth a visit.

After Greenhead the Military Road, the B6318, continues, still north of the A69, to Gilsland and the Northumberland Border. This is Milecastle Number 48 and just over the border, in Cumbria, is Birdoswald which is really the last remaining section of wall visible. Between here and Bowness on the Solway, the western terminus, there is really not much of it left. Perhaps Cumbrian farmers were more in need of building material than their Northumberland neighbours! To redress the balance it should be noted that the foundations of the Military Road contain much of The Wall.

However deep one's interest lies it has to be said that a visit to Hadrian's Wall can stir the imagination. Not only does it evoke an admiration for the skill required to construct it, but a sympathetic note is also struck when one considers the privation of manning the place in the depth of winter.

Hexham

On the A69, twenty miles wast of Newcastle.

ACTUALLY the A69 (T) bypasses the town by running north of the Tyne, thus leaving the centre less congested than previously.

The Tyne incidentally divides into the North Tyne and the South Tyne just west of Hexham, near Acomb, and a local will direct you to the bank where the confluence of these two rushing waters can be viewed.

Hexham is a sizeable place, or so it seems after touring the remoter parts of the county. Its focal point is the Abbey Church which has a colourful history and numerous items of interest which include a Saxon crypt and St. Wilfred's Chair. Like many such towns it contains a market place, a moot hall, an old grammar school and an ancient lock-up (the manor office), now serving as an Information Centre.

It is a place for browsing around with the usual assortment of the old and the new — architecturally and commercially. As a base from which this part of Northumberland can be explored it is ideal. The Wall lies to the north and west, immediately south is Blanchland and some pleasant parts of Durham and south-west lies Allendale.

Market days are the best times to visit any town if you are seeking the real atmosphere of the place. The general market is on Tuesday, whilst the equally interesting cattle and sheep market is usually Tuesdays and Fridays. Open spaces are somewhat at a premium in town centres and The Seal — a former monastic enclosure — is a popular place with both visitors and townsfolk.

Allendale — Allendale Town and Allenheads

THERE are in fact two quite separate dales lying south and east of the A686 with the two rivers, the East Allen and the West Allen, giving their names respectively to each.

It is East Allendale which is the more thickly populated, though the term is of course relative. The B6295 runs from its junction with the A686 near Langley and after Catton follows the course of the East Allen to Allenheads, then continues south to join the A689 at Cowshill.

Allendale Town lays claim to being the geographical centre of Great Britain as distinct from Meriden's claim as the centre of England. It has a quite large market square and was noted in earlier days for its proliferation of inns. The amount of accommodation available to today's tourist is quite large considering the size of the place. On New Year's Eve one of England's quaintest customs is performed by guizers who carry barrels of blazing tar on their heads.

The history of the dale is a fascinating one both socially and industrially, and today the tourist industry has replaced those earlier activities. Seven more miles up the dale is Allenheads, a village which still reflects the heyday of lead mining. Today fluorspar is mined and some skiing is attempted when the British weather obliges with an adequate supply of snow! Our Victorian forefathers saw the area as the English Alps and certainly it can be honestly described as 'scenic' with its steeply wooded slopes and rocky outcrops.

To reach the West Dale a moorland road runs off left as you return north from Allenheads. It passes bleak Killhope Law (2,056 feet), and after numerous old mine shafts descends to Coalcleugh, a village which claims, like some others, to be one of England's highest at 1,750 feet. Just a half mile south of Coalcleugh is the meeting place of Northumberland, Durham and Cumbria, one of those Three Shires locations.

Travelling north up West Allendale, Carr Shields seems a quite friendly hamlet after the bleak nature of the moors. It boasts a field study centre and a fell rescue post — there is another at Catton in the

East Dale. At Ninebanks another moorland road strikes east to link with the B6295 and the East Allen River.

It is impossible to derive the greatest pleasure from some regions without first engaging in some background reading. Allendale is one of those regions.